I0605545

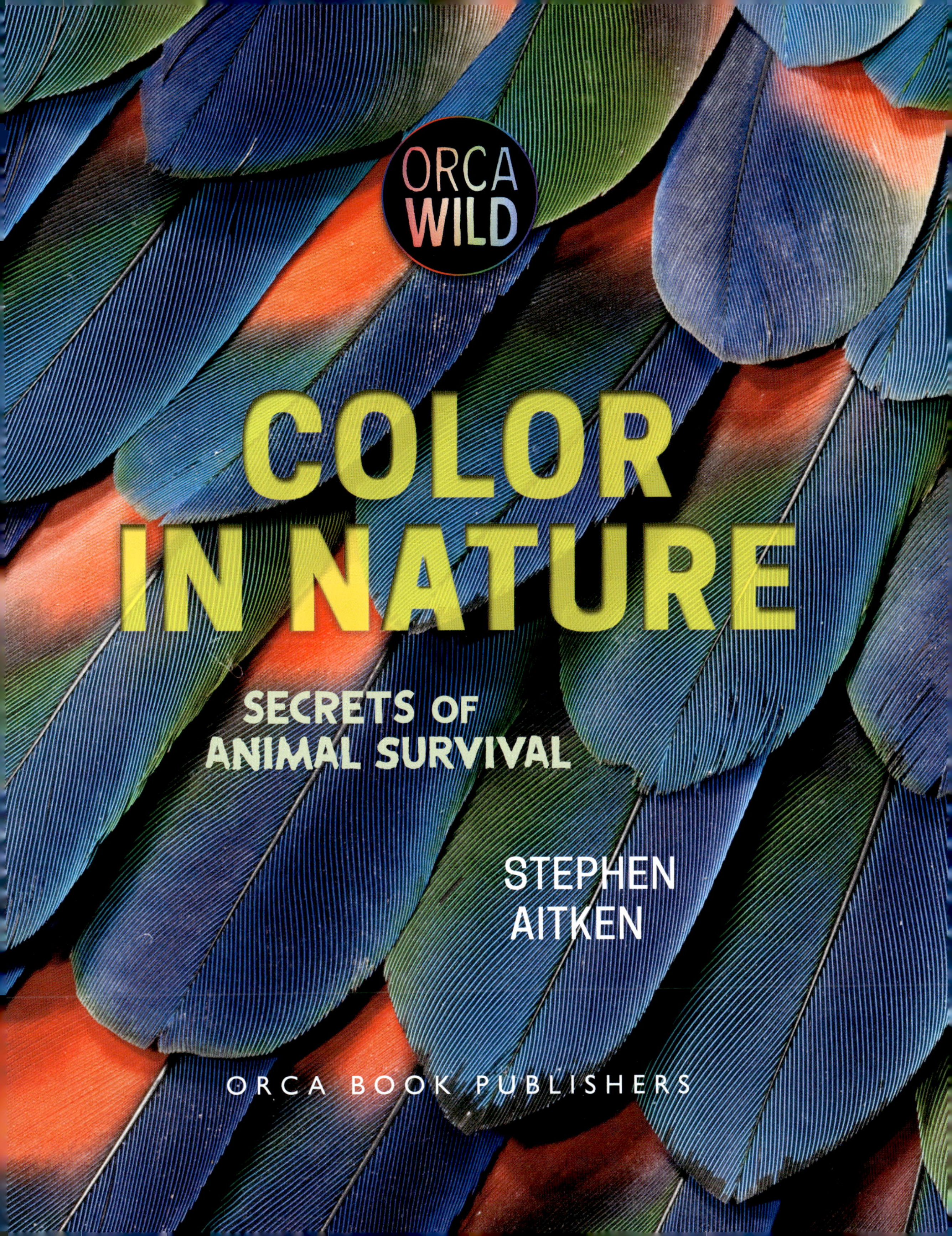
ORCA
WILD
COLOR
IN NATURE
SECRETS OF
ANIMAL SURVIVAL
STEPHEN
AITKEN
ORCA BOOK PUBLISHERS

Published in Canada and the United States in 2026 by Orca Book Publishers.

Library and Archives Canada Cataloguing in Publication
Title: Color in nature : secrets of animal survival / Stephen Aitken.
Names: Aitken, Stephen, 1953- author
Series: Orca wild ; 19.
Description: Series statement: Orca wild ; 19 | Includes bibliographical references and index.
Identifiers: Canadiana (print) 20250158604 | Canadiana (ebook) 20250158612 |
ISBN 9781459840218 (hardcover) | ISBN 9781459840225 (PDF) | ISBN 9781459840232 (EPUB)
Subjects: LCSH: Animals—Color—Juvenile literature. |
LCSH: Protective coloration (Biology)—Juvenile literature. |
LCSH: Animal behavior—Juvenile literature.
Classification: LCC QL767 .A48 2026 | DDC j591.47/2—dc23

Library of Congress Control Number: 2025933442

Summary: Part of the nonfiction Orca Wild series for middle-grade readers and illustrated with color photographs throughout, this book examines how animals use color for survival.

Orca Book Publishers is committed to reducing the consumption of nonrenewable resources in the production of our books. We make every effort to use materials that support a sustainable future.

Orca Book Publishers gratefully acknowledges the support for its publishing programs provided by the following agencies: the Government of Canada, the Canada Council for the Arts and the Province of British Columbia through the BC Arts Council and the Book Publishing Tax Credit.

Design by Troy Cunningham.
Edited by Kirstie Hudson.
Snakeskin pattern © Gunung Madjiyero
Print with monstera leaves © karandaeva.en381788

Printed and bound in South Korea.

29 28 27 26 • 1 2 3 4

ORCA BOOK PUBLISHERS
orcabook.com

To Shyam,
who opened my eyes
to a world of color

CONTENTS

Colorful food sources may contribute to the rich colors of Australian birds like this rainbow lorikeet. Australia is getting hotter and drier every year. Some experts speculate that birds' colors may help them regulate body heat.
RAFAEL BEN-ARI/GETTY IMAGES

INTRODUCTION

As spring pushes winter aside, the natural world awakens and dips its brush into a palette of colors. In the Ottawa Valley, where I was raised, meadows and hillsides are sprinkled with bluebells in late April, as delicate pastel-colored trilliums grow in small clusters on the forest floor. The first spring birds, orange-breasted robins and eastern bluebirds, flitter from tree to tree, skirting the edge of the fields. Wild shooting stars sprinkle their pink, purple and yellow flowers like bubbles along the ferned banks of the swollen brooks, spring peepers announcing their awakening. Brilliant-red cardinals and American goldfinches with their black caps appear and soon sparkle between the budding maples as white-tailed deer skip deeper into the forest in a flash of reddish-brown fur. Eastern comma and mourning cloak butterflies lift in a flutter, coming out of hiding to sprinkle oranges, yellows and blues along the patches of white snow lining the streambed.

The pink orchid mantis mimics an orchid's flower petals, helping it ambush pollinators like bees and wasps, grabbing them with its powerful front legs.
MONSTER_CODE/GETTY IMAGES

Color can be beautiful, but it is also a valuable tool. It plays a critical role in the behavior of almost every animal on Earth. The color of an animal's feathers, scales, fur or skin can be used to recognize members of one's own species, attract mates, provide a defense against rivals, hide from predators or, for predators, sneak up on prey. The color relationships in the natural world are complex and interwoven like a giant tapestry. There is so much more to the natural world than meets the human eye.

SAME BUT DIFFERENT

Animals get their color from pigments produced in their bodies or from their diets. Others are colorful because the microscopic structure of their scales, feathers and skin produces multicolored reflected light.

LIGHT AND COLOR VISION

Sunlight is the dominant source of light on Earth, but sunlight, composed of many ***wavelengths***, appears white to us. Some animals see only shades of gray because color is not useful in their world. Only when the various wavelengths within light are separated is the sensation of color perceived by the viewer. Receptors in the anatomy of the eye receive the different wavelengths of light, and the brain interprets them as different colors. But not all animals see the world around them in the same way. We humans see quite a broad range of color, but many birds and insects see more colors than we do. A lot of animals can see ***ultraviolet light*** that is outside the human visible spectrum. Some animals have specialized receptors in their eyes to see ***polarized light***. Others, such as snakes and bats, are able to see ***infrared light***, which helps them detect prey at night through its body heat.

In the animal kingdom color is used for power, attraction, distraction, deceit, warnings and even temperature regulation. Rainbow-colored birds, color-shifting chameleons, intricately patterned butterflies and snails with elaborately designed shells—all these animals use their colors in surprising ways that we are only now beginning to understand.

The more we know about how animals use color, and the more that we can see the way that they see, the more we are able to devise ways to save them *and* our colorful living planet.

> "The natural world is awash with colour, but we are only seeing half the story. If we could see things as animals do, our world would become unimaginably brighter. Now, thanks to new science and technology, we can at last open our eyes."
>
> —SIR DAVID ATTENBOROUGH, *LIFE IN COLOUR*

Using color is often interpreted as creativity to many people, like dyeing one's hair purple!
WAYRA/GETTY IMAGES

This red-eyed tree frog is able to cling to a plant in the tropical rainforest because of its sticky orange footpads. Its vibrant green body provides camouflage, while its bright red, bulging eyes serve to startle and distract predators.
PCHOUI/GETTY IMAGES

1

TEN OF THE MOST COLORFUL ANIMALS IN THE WORLD

It's a tough job to pick the 10 most colorful animals on Earth—there are just so many spectacular species to highlight. I could fill this list with birds alone. They are found all over the world, flashing a rainbow of colored feathers, beaks and legs. Butterflies are also found almost everywhere, with famously colorful and richly patterned wings. If you're near the tropical ocean, coral reefs abound with brightly colored fish, crabs and corals. This chapter includes animals from different groups—birds, insects, reptiles and amphibians that enrich the skies, oceans, deserts, grasslands, forests and mountains of our colorful planet.

THE COLORFUL KINGDOM

Birds are among the most colorful groups of animals, and you can't argue with success—there are about 10,000 bird species worldwide.

A scarlet macaw's bright colors and white-feathered face and beak help it blend into its favorite perch, which is high in the rainforest canopy.
ANDREANITA/GETTY IMAGES

Take the macaws, found in the rainforests and other areas of South America. There's the scarlet macaw, with a red body and yellow-and-blue wings. The blue-and-yellow macaw with a blue upperpart and yellow underpart. The hyacinth macaw with its cobalt-blue plumage and yellow eye-rings; the red-fronted macaw with its olive-green plumage and complementary red patches on its forehead, wings and tail; and the endangered blue-throated macaw with a turquoise-blue upper body, blue throat patch and a yellow belly. The list goes on.

Coral reefs in tropical waters are rich nurseries and breeding grounds for marine animals that are competing for survival through the brightness of their colors. Nearby tropical rainforests are also hot spots of colorful biodiversity.

This small but dangerous frog can also be green or orange in different habitats. Its toxin seeps from its skin, and even a light touch can be deadly to a predator.
TAMBAKO THE JAGUAR/GETTY IMAGES

1. GOLDEN POISON DART FROG

LOCATION: Colombia, South America

HABITAT: Tropical rainforest

COLOR ID: Stands out bright yellow against the dark green rainforest vegetation.

Its colors send a message that says, "I am one of the most toxic animals on Earth—don't you dare eat me!" A dart frog's diet of ants, termites and beetles provides it with the toxins it stores in its skin. The birds, snakes and lizards of these regions have come to know that if they chomp on one of these tiny frogs, it might be their last snack—a tiny drop of their poison can kill a human.

Many pet lovers favor brightly colored redheaded Gouldian finches. The varieties bred in captivity do not necessarily reflect the distribution of colored varieties in wild populations.
MICHEL VIARD/GETTY IMAGES

2. GOULDIAN FINCH

LOCATION: Australia

HABITAT: Savannas/open woodlands

COLOR ID: Green back, lilac breast, brilliant-yellow belly and a turquoise collar. It most commonly has a black head but some have red, orange or, less commonly, yellow heads.

This is one of Australia's most colorful birds, also known as the rainbow finch, and it's no wonder that their flocks are often referred to as treasures. These birds nest out of sight in tree cavities so their colors don't attract the attention of predators. Unlike many bird species, both the male and female are colorful.

Gouldian finches are widely bred in captivity because of high demand from the pet trade. Licenses for trappers to collect them from the wild have not been issued for 50 years, but their wild populations continue to get smaller because of ever larger, uncontrolled wildfires and the loss of their favored native grasslands due to climate and land-use change.

ME FIRST

Gouldian finches with red heads are more aggressive and usually get the first drink at local watering spots, while those with black heads shy away from fights.

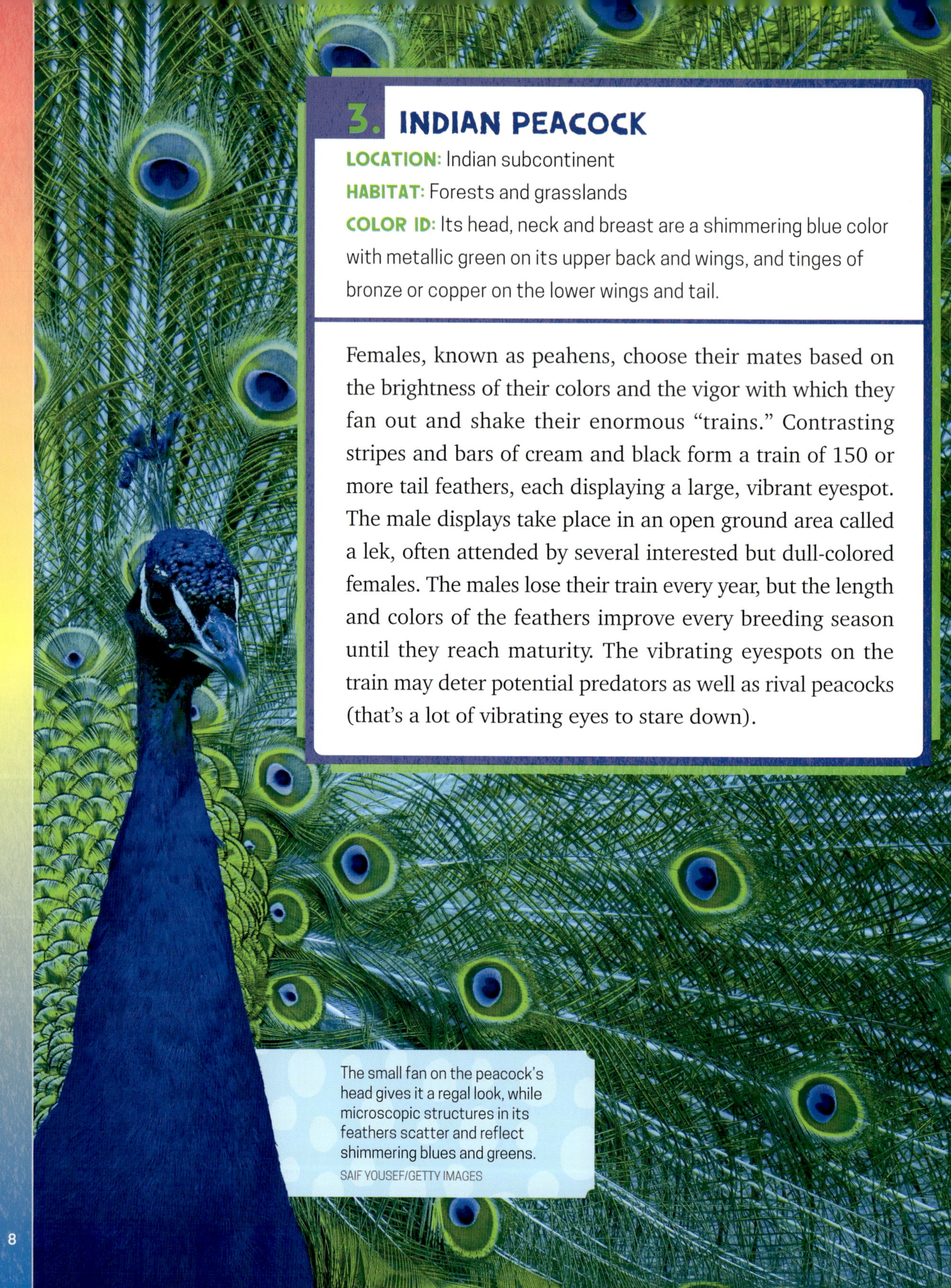

3. INDIAN PEACOCK

LOCATION: Indian subcontinent

HABITAT: Forests and grasslands

COLOR ID: Its head, neck and breast are a shimmering blue color with metallic green on its upper back and wings, and tinges of bronze or copper on the lower wings and tail.

Females, known as peahens, choose their mates based on the brightness of their colors and the vigor with which they fan out and shake their enormous "trains." Contrasting stripes and bars of cream and black form a train of 150 or more tail feathers, each displaying a large, vibrant eyespot. The male displays take place in an open ground area called a lek, often attended by several interested but dull-colored females. The males lose their train every year, but the length and colors of the feathers improve every breeding season until they reach maturity. The vibrating eyespots on the train may deter potential predators as well as rival peacocks (that's a lot of vibrating eyes to stare down).

The small fan on the peacock's head gives it a regal look, while microscopic structures in its feathers scatter and reflect shimmering blues and greens.
SAIF YOUSEF/GETTY IMAGES

The mantis shrimp's body is a mosaic of spotted and striped patterns topped by neon-colored compound eyes. Green, fanlike smashing clubs are positioned to attack prey, while other multicolored appendages help the shrimp blend into coral reefs and rocky seabed habitats.

MICHAEL GERBER/GETTY IMAGES

4. MANTIS SHRIMP

LOCATION: Tropical and subtropical oceans

HABITAT: Coral reefs, seagrass and mangroves

COLOR ID: The exact colors of each shrimp vary, and they can change colors to blend into their environment.

One of the most colorful coral reef animals, mantis shrimp use color to signal dominance over rivals, attract mates, defend their territory and disguise themselves. Instead of physical combat, this complex marine organism lets the color and size of its patterned mantle, arms and other body parts signal its dominance within the mantis population. The mantis shrimp is a true king of color.

EYES FOR COLOR

Mantis shrimp have eyes on long stalks that rotate almost a complete circle so they can see both prey and predators. Their eyes have over 12 color receptors (we have only 3), including some that see ultraviolet and polarized light. Their color vision enables them to track rival shrimp with outer shells that change to:

- **GREEN**, for hiding among seagrasses;
- **BLUE**, for mating displays (blue, after all, *is* the color of cool!);
- **RED**, for hiding in deeper waters, where red appears black;
- **YELLOW** and **ORANGE**, for communication, mating and warning off predators.

5. RAINBOW LORIKEET

LOCATION: Australia

HABITAT: Rainforests, mangroves and savannas

COLOR ID: Both the males and females sport a royal-blue head with a yellow-orange collar, an indigo-blue belly, yellow thighs and a bright red beak.

This member of the parrot family has stunning kaleidoscopic colors. The light-green feathers on their backs make them less visible to hawks hunting from above, while their richly colored undersides allow other lorikeets to identify them from below. They nest in hollowed-out cavities high up in the canopy of mature rainforests to escape predators such as monitor lizards and snakes. But when they gather in flocks and fly through urban areas, they are often classified as pests. In regions of Australia where they are not native, they invade orchards and feed on grapes, pears, apples, cherries and even vegetable crops. The lorikeet has a unique red, brush-tipped tongue that it uses to collect flower pollen and nectar, its favorite food. Some witnesses claim that when the flocks eat fermented fruit, they exhibit a pattern of drunken behavior, sometimes flying directly into buildings or other objects.

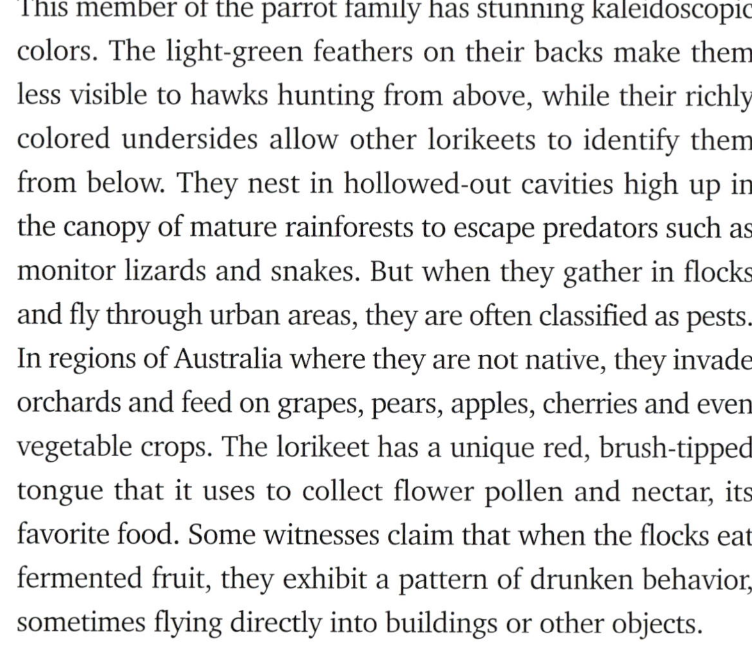

The bright colors of the rainbow lorikeet help the bird hide among colorful tropical flowers in Australia and on nearby islands. Lorikeets often puff up their feathers when threatened, making themselves appear larger and more colorful.

COLIN LANGFORD/GETTY IMAGES

Dominant male parrotfish display a variety of shimmering yellows, greens, blues, pinks and purples that help distract predators by making it difficult for them to focus on one fish.
GEORGETTE DOUWMA/GETTY IMAGES

6. PARROTFISH

LOCATION: Tropical and subtropical oceans

HABITAT: Coral reefs, seagrass and mangroves

COLOR ID: Scales pigmented with shimmering reds, blues, greens, pinks, purples and yellows

The striking patterns on the parrotfish become more vivid and complex as the fish matures. It can also change colors completely along with a change in its sex. The bright colors and complex patterns help it blend into the colorful reef environment and send signals to potential mates and rivals about its sexual maturity.

Parrotfish survive by scraping ***algae*** from rocks and corals and chewing on bits of coral, helping replenish corals that are covered in too much algae. Each parrotfish grinds out from 10 to 220 pounds (5 to 100 kilograms) of sand every year. These fish keep coral reefs healthy and colorful and at the same time help make the lovely white sand of tropical beaches. They develop a protective mucous cocoon around their bodies at night that helps hide their colorful bodies.

7. JUMPING SPIDERS

LOCATION: All continents (except Antarctica)

HABITAT: All environments

COLOR ID: Browns, grays, blues, purples, greens and reds

These spiders jump out (in more ways than one) from other spider groups for their elaborate body patterns and excellent vision. They can leap distances up to 50 times their own body length, making them ferocious hunters. If you were a jumping spider, you could jump three times the length of your school gym from a standing position! Of course, you would also have four sets of spider eyes, including a large forward-facing pair with excellent focus and color perception.

There are more than 6,000 recorded species of jumping spiders. The male peacock spider from Australia is not much bigger than a grain of rice and has fanlike flaps that extend the colorful designs on its abdomen (like the train of a peacock). Females find the male's shimmering blue, red, orange, yellow and green colors very impressive. The flaps contain eyespots (like the peacock's), an important part of its color pattern. During the courtship display the male repeatedly raises and lowers his colorful abdomen while waving a pair of legs vigorously in the air. The female prefers the most colorful and vigorous dancer for her male partner, often eating unsuccessful suitors. Talk about performance pressure!

A male peacock spider displays his abdomen flaps with their intricate red-and-blue design. The patterns and colors vary between species, and when not in use the flaps fold neatly against the spider's body.
ROBBIE GOODALL/GETTY IMAGES

8. MANDARIN FISH

LOCATION: Indo-Pacific Ocean

HABITAT: Coral reefs

COLOR ID: Brightly decorated in blues, greens, oranges and yellows

Mandarin is a reference to the similarity between the colors of the fish and the robes worn by scholars in Imperial China. Though small at about two inches (five centimeters), each individual provides a form of reef ***camouflage*** that makes this species very popular in the aquarium trade. Their brilliant blue fins and striped scaleless bodies contain special cells called ***cyanophores*** that are rich in blue pigment.

During the mandarin's twilight mating ritual, the male raises his spiny dorsal fin to warn rivals away and invite an interested female, smaller in size, to snuggle up and sit on his pelvic fin. The two vibrantly colored lovers then rise in the waters cheek-to-cheek, fins aflutter, while releasing a flurry of several hundred ***gametes*** (eggs and sperm). Following their courtship dance, their colors soon pale, and the couple settles down to blend into the reef floor.

The mandarin fish, one of the most vibrantly colored fish in the ocean, is a distant relative of the seahorse. Its psychedelic colors, made from nanostructures in its skin, are a warning to predators that they are toxic.
KHOROSHUNOVA OLGA/SHUTTERSTOCK.COM

The keel-billed toucan's bright colors keep it hidden as it gulps down tropical fruit whole. The toucan helps regenerate forests by regurgitating the seeds later.
ANDY MORFFEW/WIKIMEDIA COMMONS/CC BY 2.0

9. THE KEEL-BILLED TOUCAN

LOCATION: Central and South America

HABITAT: Tropical rainforests

COLOR ID: It has a bill of blue, red, orange and green, a sulfur-yellow head, neck and breast and a dark black body.

Also known as the rainbow-billed toucan, the keel-billed toucan is the national bird of Belize. Its vibrant colors are intended to impress mates and show dominance to rivals. Its large flattened bill has a sharp edge along the top like the keel of a boat.

Fortunately (for the bird), the bill is quite light, as it is made of hollow bone wrapped in ***keratin***. As it flies from one tree to another, the toucan appears to be pushing a striped banana forward. The bill is a useful tool for grabbing high-hanging fruit and digging into crevices for insects and lizards, and it is also not unusual to see the male bird using his bill in a fencing duel with a rival male to defend his territory. Toucans nest in tree holes as a way of keeping their colorful beaks hidden, several toucans managing to fit inside a single abandoned woodpecker hole, their beaks tucked under their wings for protection as they sleep. (Oh, to be a toucan while traveling economy on international flights!)

10. PANTHER CHAMELEON

LOCATION: Madagascar

HABITAT: Tropical forests

COLOR ID: The color range of the species includes bright red, yellow, orange, turquoise, sky and marine blue and a variety of rich greens.

The panther chameleon from Madagascar, one of the most colorful chameleon species, is an aggressive predatorial lizard (as you might have guessed by the name). It hisses angrily at any approaching danger and quickly changes colors to defend its territory.

The male anatomy includes knobby skin that runs along the back, ending in a ridged crest on the head. If color messaging fails, only then will he resort to physical combat. After a male loses a battle, his colors quickly fade as he retreats. Females also use their color-changing skills, brightening up during courtship periods and then dimming down their colors after mating. A chameleon's colors can also help conceal their outline against background vegetation, making it more difficult for predators to target them. The chameleon's small, bulbous eyes that rotate independently have excellent color and ultraviolet (UV) light vision that helps them spot prey from as far away as 30 feet (9 meters).

The panther chameleon moves with a slow swaying motion, like the breeze. Its long, sticky tongue can dart out a distance of twice its body length to grab crickets, grasshoppers and flies. You have to be pretty fast to catch a fly!
STEFAN HUWILER/GETTY IMAGES

How do the feathers, scales, fur and skin of animals become colored in the first place? Why do some animals not change color at all while others go through rapid color transitions? It all has to do with pigments, microscopic structures and ***biochemistry***. Let's head over to the animal studio and take a closer look at how (and why) they do it.

There are six species of flamingos, found on five continents. They often feed in the thousands on salt flats or in lagoons where few predators survive. A flamingo's bill has a unique shape that helps it filter food out of the water.
JOHNER IMAGES/GETTY IMAGES

2 ANIMAL STUDIO: MAKING COLOR FROM LIGHT

The first signs of color in the animal world appeared about 600 million years ago when multicellular organisms evolved pigments to protect themselves from the harsh rays of the sun. A hundred million years later, the first eyes evolved. Soon after that color receptors appeared that enabled animals to distinguish colors. Today vibrant colors are found across all five major vertebrate animal groups—mammals, birds, reptiles, amphibians and fish—as well as in insects and spiders.

What a dull world it would be without their rich color palettes! The colors that an animal produces are influenced by how they see the world and how they are seen by their prey and their own predators.

COLORS AND CONES

Sunlight contains a whole range of wavelengths of light that includes the colors of the rainbow, from violet to red. Specialized receptors in animal

A large pronghorn buck in Montana. The inserted circle represents the colors these herbivores see with their dichromatic vision.
JARED LLOYD/GETTY IMAGES

eyes (including humans') can detect the different wavelengths and send signals to the brain to create the sensation of color. Humans, for example, have trichromatic vision—we have three different color receptors (known as cones) sensitive to the blue, green and red wavelengths of light. Looking at a rainbow, our eyes see seven major colors: red, orange, yellow, green, blue, indigo and violet (I remember them by imagining a friend named ROY G BIV).

ALL THE COLORS

Pronghorn antelopes have ***dichromatic vision*** and, like most mammals (other than humans), they don't see red and orange. The receptor cells in their eyes only respond to blue and green wavelengths of light. However, their eyes are very sensitive to movement, helping them spot predators at a great distance.

A hawk on the other hand, like many birds, sees in tetracolor. It has three color receptors sensitive to red, green and blue *and* a fourth receptor that sees ultraviolet light. UV vision enables raptors like hawks to track prey that leave UV-reflecting urine trails as they move through the landscape. Many reptiles, amphibians, fish and insects are also sensitive to UV light. They use this special power to hunt for food, avoid predators and, in some species, select suitable mates.

The ability of animals to see color has evolved hand in hand with their ability to create color. So how do they do it?

A red-shouldered hawk is chased by a purple martin defending its nest. The red, green and blue colors of the circle represent the hawk's tetrachromatic vision, but our eyes can't see the "secret color" of the UV light, which is beyond violet in the color spectrum.
MICHAEL J. COHEN/GETTY IMAGES

PIGMENT POWER

The word *pigment* is derived from the Latin verb *pingere,* meaning "to paint or color." Artists use pigments every day, some mixed with oil, plastic or even water, to help them paint their ideas. ***Pigmentation*** is common in animal coloration (though they don't actually paint it on). Where do pigments come from? Some pigments are made through an animal's own biochemistry, while others come through their food. The most common types of pigments in animals are the melanins and ***carotenoids*** (think carrots) and, to a lesser extent (weird word alert!), porphyrins and pteridines. These pigments are responsible for the colors red, orange, yellow, green, blue, brown and black, absorbing some wavelengths of light and reflecting others. The reflected light is perceived as the animal's color through the eyes of the viewer.

MELANIN

The most common pigment is melanin. It is stored in special cells, called melanocytes, found in the skin, eyes, hair and certain parts of the brains of mammals and birds. Melanin is responsible for variations in the color of skin, hair and feathers and plays a role in protecting animals (including people) from the harmful effects of sunlight by absorbing and scattering some of the sun's UV radiation.

In reptiles, amphibians and fish, melanin-producing cells are called melanophores. These cells have long arms that can spread the melanin across the skin. When melanin spreads out over skin (or scales), the surface becomes darker, and when it pulls back to the center of the cell, the surface appears lighter. This enables animals to make quick color changes in response to their environment.

This textured pebbly surface is a close-up view of a chameleon's skin. Layers of specialized cells reflect and scatter light into different colors by shifting tiny cell structures according to the emotional state of the lizard.

ISAAC74/GETTY IMAGES

A juvenile American flamingo is covered in gray and white down feathers. The chicks eat regurgitated food from their parents and practice scooping water with their curved beaks in preparation for a diet of shrimp and algae.
TANE-MAHUTA/GETTY IMAGES

EAT YOUR CAROTENOIDS

Carotenoids are pigments involved in plant (including algae) photosynthesis, the process by which plants convert sunlight into energy. Animals get carotenoids through eating fruit, vegetables, algae or bacteria, which produce the bright red, orange and yellow colors seen in many animals. They also help boost immune systems and lower the risk of disease. This is a good reason to eat colorful salads along with your meals—after all, we also belong to the animal kingdom!

Porphyrins are other pigments that produce reds, browns and greens in the feathers of birds and the scales of certain reptiles. Animals don't need to eat anything special to get porphyrins. They are made in their own bodies, where they help oxygen move through the animal's blood. Another pigment group, pteridines, are also made by the animals themselves, producing the yellows and reds seen in the skin and eyes of some amphibians, fish and reptiles.

PASSING ALONG THE PINK

When I traveled to Africa as a young man, I stayed for a while in Essaouira, on the coast of Morocco. Every morning I ran along the beach through large flocks of pink flamingos feeding along the water's edge. I noticed that some of the birds were much pinker than others. Flamingos get their pink color from a diet of red shrimp and other small crustaceans. Flamingo chicks are born completely white. Flamingos can't make pink and neither can shrimp, but when shrimp eat algae, their carotenoid pigments accumulate in their bodies. The flamingo's digestive system breaks down the carotenoids in the shrimp and stores them in its feathers, skin and beak, turning them pink. A vibrant pink color is treasured by both males and females when choosing a mate. However, it takes close to five years of a carotenoid-rich diet (that's a lot of shrimp) to get that beautiful flamingo pink.

MICROCOLOR

In the cabinets at the Canadian National Collection of Insects, Arachnids and Nematodes (CNC) in Ottawa, there are more than 120,000 species of beetles collected from around the world, such as brilliant jewel beetles and shimmering scarabs. Over the period I worked there, I saw that their shining colors never seemed to fade, even decades after they were collected. Unlike pigmented colors that rely on biochemical compounds, structural color is produced by tiny structures embedded in surfaces like the hard wing covers (the elytra) of beetles or the scales of butterfly wings, fish and other marine animals. Structural color is "built in," so it does not fade easily. Often the microstructures break the incoming light into different wavelengths and reflect it back to the viewer as ***iridescent*** color, like those in a peacock feather and many butterfly wings. Other arrangements reflect the light back as a single solid color, like the blue feathers of a blue jay.

This eye-catching leaf beetle reflects metallic colors that shift between green, blue, gold and copper. Its colors have multiple functions: providing camouflage, warning of toxicity (from its feeding on dogbane and milkweed plants) and attracting mates.
MARIANNA ARMATA/GETTY IMAGES

PUTTING IT ALL TOGETHER

Are there some animals who take advantage of both pigmented *and* structural color? You bet there are! Chameleons are the master colorists of the animal kingdom, capable of rapidly changing their different body parts from dull brown to bright blue, red, orange or yellow, and they do it using both pigments and microstructures. But how do they do it so quickly? The answer is in the skin—all four layers of it! The surface layer of most chameleons is largely transparent, but the underlying layers contain yellow and red pigments and melanin (which adds the colors brown and black).

The veiled chameleon has a pair of the most advanced eyes in the reptile world. Pinhole-like pupils are set in the middle of cone-shaped eyes that rotate independently, enabling it to quickly find and focus on insect prey.
TIM PLATT/GETTY IMAGES

EMOTIONAL COLOR

Chameleons often appear green in their relaxed state, a result of blue structural color mixing with yellow pigments in the upper layers. But when they're excited, they often exhibit more vivid colors, like oranges and reds.

The blue-green breast shield of the male superb bird-of-paradise is made of specialized feathers that form a cape-like shape during mating displays. Recent research shows that some species emit a fluorescent glow to enhance their displays.
GAVRIEL JECAN/GETTY IMAGES

The real magic happens in the tiny ***nanocrystals*** the chameleon rearranges for different color effects that reflect back through the upper layers. This sophisticated, layered approach to color enables the chameleon, as well as some other animals, like cuttlefish and anole lizards, to make dramatic color changes.

SUPER BLACK AND THE POWER OF CONTRAST

As an artist I have discovered that painting an area of pure black around a colored area can draw attention to the color and make it appear even brighter. Some animals know this too.

- The male superb bird-of-paradise captures the attention of a potential mate with his jet-black body and spread wings that act as a backdrop to enhance the vibrant blue-green colors of his breast shield.
- Wasps and bees use the strong contrast between black and yellow to warn off predators.
- Research shows that some jet-black colors contain nanocrystals that act like little light vacuums, absorbing 99.5 percent of the light striking them. This principle has been used by researchers at MIT to develop the blackest black ever made, even darker than Vantablack. It absorbs 99.995 percent of the visible light that strikes it and is being applied to the design of optical instruments like space telescopes to produce sharper images. Super black alone can also help some animals like the velvet spider, and "Vantablack" fish hide in the darkness of their habitats.

COLOR CURRENTS

If you wear a black T-shirt on a sunny day, you may feel warmer than if you wear a white one (try it for yourself). Black absorbs more incoming light energy, while white reflects it. Monarch butterflies make use of this basic principle. A study published in the journal *Nature* showed that the longest-distance migrating monarchs between Canada and Mexico had white spots on their wings 3 percent larger than those that traveled shorter distances. This is no small percentage—it can mean the difference between life and death. The black and white spots provide energy-saving lift through air currents, enabling the monarch to fly up to 100 miles (160 kilometers) a day. The high contrast between white and black areas causes swirling pockets of air that help the paper-thin wings stay afloat. This principle is now being applied by engineers designing drones to help make them fly more efficiently.

CARLOS. E. SERRANO/GETTY IMAGES

Two fireflies light up on a leaf in Japan, where fireflies are part of a rich cultural tradition. Many Japanese poems relate the short bursts of firefly light to the fleeting nature of life, and fireflies are thought to embody the souls of departed loved ones.
TOMOSANG/GETTY IMAGES

BIOLUMINESCENT LIGHT AND COLOR

Fireflies produce their yellow-green light from chemicals in their bodies. Like a glow stick flashing on and off, their light is timed to attract females of their own species. In deep ocean waters, as many as three out of four animals are ***bioluminescent***, their luminous colors ranging from shades of blue to green and red. In the ocean, longer-wavelength (lower-energy) red light gets absorbed quickly in surface waters. Shorter-wavelength blue light penetrates deeper, which is why the ocean appears blue from the surface. Most marine animals have no receptors in their eyes for seeing red light because they don't need them. Some fish take advantage of this and produce red light to use for hunting unsuspecting prey that can't see them coming.

UV AND WHAT WE DON'T SEE

Ultraviolet light is high-energy light with a short wavelength. We can't see it, but as we've discovered, many birds, reptiles, fish, butterflies and bees have UV-sensitive receptors in their eyes—and they use it like a superpower.

- UV-reflective patterns on the feathers of some birds help them communicate and flash their advertisements to potential mates like neon signs that say, "I'm healthy and strong—choose me!"
- Honeybees use their UV vision to detect nectar guides, which are UV patterns found on the surface of flower petals that act like a landing strip, leading the bees to the nectar and pollen.
- Some field mice have UV-sensitive eyes that help them see the dark silhouette of a hawk in flight (its feathers do not reflect UV light) against the UV-rich sky. A few seconds' advantage can help the rodents survive by avoiding fast-approaching predators.
- Caribou use their UV vision to find food during long Arctic winters, quickly locating moss and ***lichen*** against UV-rich snow.

COLOR CLUE

FLUORESCENCE

Fluorescent animals such as many beetles and birds appear luminous, but they do not make their own light. They change the energy of the incoming light and reflect it back as a glowing color, like natural glow sticks.

Some wild geranium species have UV nectar guides, with parts of the flower absorbing UV light while others reflect it, creating a bull's-eye effect that guides bees directly to its nectar.
MANFREDXY/GETTY IMAGES

A mandrill with its ridged blue and red nose. Mature mandrill males compete for dominance in their hordes, which can reach over a thousand individuals in size.

JOHN W. BANAGAN/GETTY IMAGES

3 MAKING AN IMPRESSION: MATING AND DOMINANCE

Every animal needs to attract a mate. In order to stand out from the crowd, the male of the species often develops exaggerated colors. Wearing a colorful outfit is a powerful way to get attention. The brilliance of his feathers, scales or skin is a way to show the female that he can produce strong offspring and provide food and protection. The duller colors of many females can help them blend into their habitat while they nurture their young.

The courtship displays and performances by birds, insects and other animals are some of the most fascinating behaviors in the animal kingdom. For example, the vigorous pole dance of the male bird-of-paradise ends with the flashy display of his shiny breastplate. The hooded seal, on the other hand, exudes a bright red sac of loose skin (known as a "hood") out of his left nostril in one of nature's most bizarre (and strangely effective) mating rituals. These displays and behaviors, in addition to highlighting the health and fitness of the male, help females recognize members of their own species.

COUNTING CLOWNFISH

Studies show that marine animals also rely on colors and patterns to identify members of their own species. There are about 30 species of clownfish, a colorful coral reef animal, and each species varies in size, color and number of stripes. The most common type are the "Nemo" fish, with bold white stripes on bright orange bodies. They aggressively defend their territory from rivals. Japanese researchers used painted resin decoys to show that male clownfish can clearly count the vertical stripes of intruders to determine their species. The study showed that male clownfish were much more aggressive toward rival males with the same number of stripes as themselves.

VOJCE/GETTY IMAGES

Guenon monkeys have diverse facial features that reduce competition and interbreeding between closely related species. This individual has distinctive blue facial skin, a white nose and light cheek tufts.
HOLLY CANNON/GETTY IMAGES

YOUR COLOR IDs, PLEASE!

Evolution does not typically favor reproduction between closely related species—the offspring (known as hybrids) are often unhealthy and have a low survival rate. For example, the mule is a hybrid offspring of a male donkey and a female horse (mare). Though it is strong and capable of working, it is sterile and can't reproduce—resulting in an evolutionary dead end.

To prevent interspecies breeding, animals identify each other through clear visual cues, including color. Many primates, like the guenon, a group of about two dozen species of primates in sub-Saharan Africa, use facial features to identify peers and detect rivals. These monkeys have highly complex social structures, and the different species recognize each other by their eye tufts and the colors displayed on their faces. Remarkably, golden paper wasps can even identify individual hive members by their facial markings, a highly advanced skill for an insect. We humans also use color and other visual cues to recognize friends and acquaintances.

STANDING OUT

As we've discovered, the peacock is a classic example of ***sexual dimorphism***, which means the male and female of the same species have distinctly different colors and appearances. Many birds exhibit radical color differences between genders. Take, for example, the male yellow-beaked, bright green eclectus parrot found in South Pacific rainforests. The female is black-beaked, has purple/blue underwings and belly, and a deep-red head, neck and chest. They look like two different species—but they're not. The brightly colored females nest in dark tree hollows, where they disappear in the darkness. The females are as fierce as their fiery red feathers, ready to defend their nests to the death. The green upper bodies of the males provide camouflage from raptors flying through the canopy above, hunting for food.

A male eclectus parrot with blue wing patches and tail feathers, and a brilliant red female. The males are generally more affectionate, calm and sociable, while the females are more dominant and territorial.
ANG HWEE YONG/GETTY IMAGES

The vivid blue eyespots on the upper wing surfaces are the inspiration for the peacock butterfly's name. Its underwings provide camouflage, but if it is threatened, this butterfly produces a hissing sound by rubbing its wings together.
CANSON/GETTY IMAGES

FLASHING JEWELS

Butterflies, like birds, have the advantage of wings with two distinct surfaces. When the wings are closed above the insect's body, the colors on the underside of the wings can help them blend into their environment. Opened during flight, the upper wing surfaces can send colored messages to impress mates or warn off predators. For example, the peacock butterfly, found in many European parks and gardens, stays hidden with dark mottled colors on the undersides of its wings. But the upper surfaces of its wings are a rich rusty red with bright blue eyespots that stand out against the green foliage of its habitat as it flies. Its colors serve to impress mates and dominate rivals by exhibiting the insect's fitness and strength. Research indicates that females prefer a male with large, bright blue eyespots.

BLUE THROATS AND FIRE BELLIES

Amphibians also exhibit sexual dimorphism, the males developing brighter and richer colors during mating season. Salamanders, toads, newts and frogs, all members of the class Amphibia, use their colors to attract mates and establish dominance. Many frogs brighten their colors to signal readiness to mate, dominate rivals and help defend their territories.

For example:

- Male red-eyed tree frogs in Central America make their green, yellow and black markings even brighter during breeding season.
- Male moor frogs develop intense blue throats during mating season—the richer the blue, the higher the appeal to females.
- Newts get fire in their bellies to mate. Male Asian fire-bellied newts develop an orange-red belly with black body markings.

Once breeding season comes to an end, colors typically fade, and amphibians blend back into the wetlands as their offspring emerge.

The large red eyes and vertical pupils of this tree frog can startle predators, providing time for it to escape. Tree frogs can also shake tree branches with their webbed toes and orange footpads to warn off rival males.
DAN MIHAI/GETTY IMAGES

The bright red belly of this newt warns predators of its toxicity, while its dark-colored upper body helps it avoid detection when at rest. It adds to its warning message with an unken reflex, arching its back and limbs to display normally hidden bright colors.
IPPEI NAOI/GETTY IMAGES

The Vogelkop superb bird-of-paradise, a close relative of the superb bird-of-paradise that is famous for its "smiley face" dance routine, has its own signature moves and colored accessories to attract females. But it's known for its frowny-face display.
JJ HARRISON/WIKIMEDIA COMMONS/CC BY-SA 4.0

BIRDS: TURNING ON THE COLOR CHARM

The male bird-of-paradise from New Guinea puts on a colorful pole-dancing courtship. After clearing an area of distracting debris, he perches on a branch in full view of the females below, like an acrobat on a high wire. A cobalt-blue bill contrasts with a reddish-brown crown as the male vibrates wiry blue-green tail feathers while clinging to his perch with neon blue legs, like a dancer riding a pole. The bird's act reaches its climax when he puffs up his brilliant iridescent-green breast shield within a frame of jet black, forming a Batman-like cape. Ta-da! This act is one of the most colorful courting displays in the animal kingdom and serves to show how animals, birds in particular, can use dramatic behaviors (like pole dancing) to bring attention to their colorful plumage.

A BLUE-FOOTED BOOBY DANCE

Boobies are expert divers, reaching up to 60 miles per hour (100 kilometers per hour) as they dive into sardine- and mackerel-rich waters off the Pacific coast. But male blue-footed boobies also put on a colorful dance to encourage females to join them on the dance floor. A male booby will often present a female with a stick or stone as a gift and then do a circular little dance that's all about showing off his blue legs. In a final flourish he spreads his wings, raises his beak in the air and lets out a series of shrill whistles into the sky (what's a dance without a song?). If the female is impressed, she dances in step with the male and stretches her wings out in a gesture of praise for his great performance—a fitting finale to a musical performance deserving of a place on Broadway.

Boobies get their colored pigments from the food they eat along with structures in the skin of their legs and feet that reflect and intensify the blue color. If they can't catch fish, their legs start losing color within days.

Blue-footed boobies on the Galápagos Islands of Ecuador have a slightly comical look, but their high aerial dives into ocean waters are no joke. Females choose mates who have the brightest blue feet to ensure the strongest offspring.
ADRIAN WOJCIK/GETTY IMAGES

Different species of bowerbirds look for different colors for decorating, but their thieving ways seem to be a common bowerbird trait. They constantly rearrange the objects in their displays to create the optical illusion that they are the biggest bird of all.

(MAIN) LUKE SHELLEY/SHUTTERSTOCK.COM; (INSET) JOAO INACIO/GETTY IMAGES

BOWERS: A DRAMA IN BLUE

The blue colors found in the feathers of many birds are created by microscopic structures that reflect blue light. The male satin bowerbird creates a whole drama around the color blue and provides a rare example of an animal building a physical structure to set the stage for courtship. This Australian bowerbird has shiny black plumage with an iridescent sheen, highlighted by bright blue eyes. He builds a dome-shaped "bower" of twigs and branches, designed to lead the female's attention down an avenue to the "stage" at the other end. The male bird carefully arranges a collection of decorative objects (even if he has to steal them from other bowers)—flowers, fruit, snail shells, ballpoint-pen tops, bottle caps, straws and even clothespins—all blue! When a female approaches the bower, the male struts onto the stage in full dance, accompanied by loud cries directed toward the sky, his wings spread wide. If the olive-green female looks distracted, he adds more drama by picking up a blue object in his beak and repeating the entire performance just to impress her!

THE COLOR OF AGGRESSION

The use of color and design to dominate rivals can be seen throughout the animal kingdom. Vibrant color can intimidate other males without the need for physical combat. For example, the male great tit (a European bird) is a brilliant yellow. His yellow breast is dissected by a black bib-like design that extends down from the bird's head and neck. The length and width of the black bib is a clear sign of dominance—the bigger and wider it is, the more likely a rival male will back off from a possible conflict.

PRIMATES: BLUE-NOSED MANDRILLS

Primates are often dull in color, with gray, silver or brown fur. But bare skin on their faces and other body parts can display bright reds and blues that emphasize facial features due to red blood cells visible through the bare skin.

One of the most dramatic examples of facial (and butt) coloration occurs in mandrills, primates that live in the forests of West Africa. A mature male mandrill is three times the size of the average female. He sports a long, bright red nose with powder blue along the length of each side of his nose. A blue rump serves to highlight a bright red tail (apparently blue butts are very impressive to female mandrills) completing a message that says, "I am strong, healthy and ready to mate." The striking blues and reds are achieved by ***chromatophores*** (pigment-containing cells) in the skin and tiny structures that reflect blue light. The colored markings indicate a male's social status when troops of mandrills join up to form a horde. When a male loses a fight for dominance or runs away from a conflict, his colors rapidly begin to fade.

LIPSTICK ON A MONKEY

As mating season approaches, dominant male black-and-white snub-nosed monkeys develop bright ruby-red lips that stand out against their pinkish cheeks and flattened noses. This sends a strong message to rival males: "This is my territory *and* my ***harem*** of females!"

A male mandrill displays his bright red tail and blue rump. These colors are controlled by hormones, specifically testosterone, in the case of the male. A defeated rival dulls in color because of a drop in his hormone levels.
GEORGECLERK/GETTY IMAGES

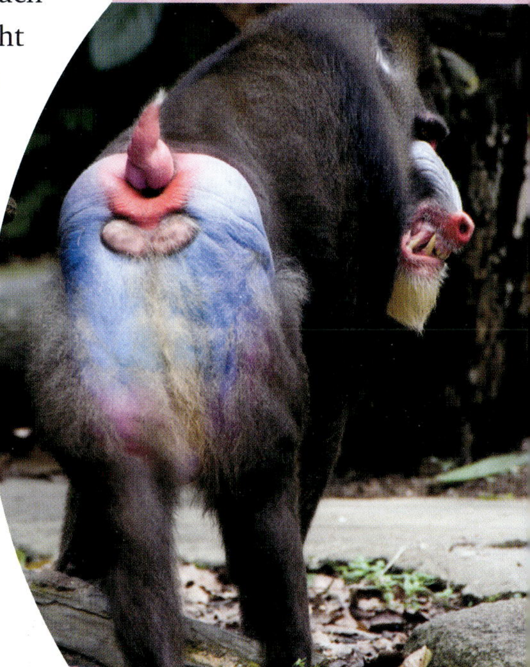

FORGET ME NOT!

Sometimes being colorful is not about impressing a mate or a rival. It's about getting well-needed care and pampering. Adult silvered langurs, found in the forests of Southeast Asia, have gray fur all over their bodies. Female langurs give birth to a single baby per breeding season. But that baby stands out in a troop of about 30 silvery gray adults because it has brilliant golden-orange fur. It quickly becomes the center of attention, with young mothers often fighting over who gets to hold and nurse the new baby. Some research indicates that the golden color may also help camouflage the babies in the dappled sunlight of the forest canopy, hiding the young monkey's outline and reducing its visibility to raptors hunting from above, and to leopards, snakes and lizards below. At about six months of age, the golden fur of the young langur starts to fade, slowly turning to gray. Soon another golden newborn appears and quickly takes over as the center of attention.

FIONA ROGERS/GETTY IMAGES

LIZARDS: DEWLAPS AND PUSH-UPS

Sometimes you just need the right accessory to complete an outfit, like a lovely red scarf over a green holiday sweater. Anoles, lizards of the genus *Anolis*, have their own built-in accessories. They live in the Caribbean and South America, some dwelling on forest floors, others living in the trees. Forest-floor lizards are often brownish in color to blend in with dried leaves and decaying matter, while the tree dwellers are shades of green, colors that help them hide between the fresh leaves above. Anole lizards have a unique piece of anatomy—a colorful flap of skin called a dewlap that extends from under the chin to the chest (like a retractable bib for messy eaters). The dewlaps come in an assortment of colors and patterns, and they help male lizards stand out from their rivals. Orange-red is the color of choice for lizards in bright environments, and yellow for those in darker forest habitats. When rival males meet, both males bob their bodies up and down (as if doing push-ups), aggressively displaying their dewlaps. The female's dewlap is much smaller, pinker and less conspicuous in color.

A male green anole lizard displays his reddish-orange dewlap, or throat fan. In front of rivals, males bob their heads (and dewlaps) vigorously, but in front of females, they make much slower, controlled movements.
MARIANNA ARMATA/GETTY IMAGES

UNDER COVER

Not all animals want to use their colors to make an impression to attract mates or repel rivals. For many it is important to blend into their environment to escape being eaten by predators while other animals want to remain unseen to sneak up on their prey.

Is it a leaf or an insect? Leaf insects from the family Phylliidae have an incredible ability to mimic the shapes and colors of leaves in order to hide themselves in vegetation.
SOMNUK KROBKUM/GETTY IMAGES

4

THE ART OF INVISIBILITY: NOW YOU SEE ME... NOW YOU DON'T

From forests to deserts, wetlands to tundra, grasslands to aquatic habitats (freshwater and marine), animals live in a wide range of habitats in the natural world. Many animals use camouflage to hide themselves and disguise their behavior. The cobalt blue tarantula is almost invisible on the dark rainforest floor of Southeast Asia, the black spots on the cheetah's body keep it well hidden in African grasslands, a mucus-covered green moray eel blends into its seagrass environment seamlessly, and only a keen trained eye can spot a ghost tiger beetle as it races over a North American sand dune. These are a few examples of how camouflage is an important survival strategy for many animals.

THE COLOR OF COOPERATION

Many animals have evolved their colors through a process known as ***adaptive evolution***—the development over time of characteristics such as color that help a species survive as their environment changes.

To hide, great potoos like this female and juvenile can remain very still, close their eyes into slits, tilt their heads upright and develop feathers that resemble lichen or fungus-covered bark.
SYLVAIN CORDIER/GETTY IMAGES

A male ruby-throated hummingbird displays his bright metallic throat colors to dazzle and impress females and intimidate rivals. Tiny structures in these birds' feathers make their heads and backs appear green, making them less visible to predators like hawks.
CAVAN IMAGES/GETTY IMAGES

For example, the color of many birds matches the color of the flowers they visit for nectar or the places where they perch.

- The ruby-throated hummingbird's bright red throat patch is the same color as its favorite cardinal flower.
- The variable sunbird has fiery-red plumage that matches its favorite nectar source, the firecracker plant.
- The South American great potoo takes camouflage to an extreme level. This bird's entire body matches the colors and texture of the branches and tree stumps on which it perches.

DISAPPEARING ACT

There are also many examples of camouflage colors that have evolved to match the particular behaviors of animals in their habitats. For example, the upper wing surfaces of the blue morpho butterfly have an intense blue color that is visible only when it flutters through the tropical jungle. The undersurfaces of its wings are brown, helping the butterfly disappear against the jungle ground cover when it is at rest. Forest floors are also home to rodents like chipmunks, deer mice and rats. Their fur colors are not accidental—they match the ground where they feed and scurry about. In Africa the yellow mongoose has evolved a special yellow-orange color that matches the unique sand of its dune habitat, hiding it from hawks, jackals and lions while it stalks its own prey of small animals and birds.

The emerald glass frog almost disappears when it rests on the surface of a leaf during the day. It is mostly active at night, when dim lighting makes its transparency even more effective.
RAINER MUELLER/GETTY IMAGES

THE TRANSPARENCY TRICK

The emerald glass frog has come up with a novel solution to camouflaging itself—invisibility! By minimizing the color of its body, this frog disappears into its background as light passes right through its body. The belly of the glass frog is transparent (the heart, stomach and other organs are visible inside its body), so there is very little shadow when it sits on a leaf. The top of this tree-dwelling frog has some green coloration with yellow spots, which helps it blend into the forest foliage when viewed from above by hawks and owls. Similarly, the glasswing butterfly relies on see-through wings to hide from predators while it flutters through the rainforest. The transparent sections of its wings are largely free of the scales and pigments that give most butterflies their color, allowing light to pass through.

Marine environments are the perfect habitat for animals that rely on their glass-like surfaces to remain hidden. Down deep you'll find glass squid, glass octopuses and transparent species of both shrimp and comb jellies.

EXCUSE YOU

One of the insect world's weirdest (and grossest) adaptations is found in the alder moth caterpillar. When threatened, the shape and color of its entire body suddenly transforms into what looks like a heap of bird droppings. Ewww! That would certainly keep me away if I were a predator.

BUG ABILITIES

Insects are one of the most successful groups of animals on Earth. They're really good at surviving because they can adapt in so many ways, including by the use of color and pattern. One example is an amazing family of insects called Phylliidae, or "walking leaves." They look just like real leaves—some even have patterns that make them look like they've been nibbled on by animals. This helps them blend in and avoid being eaten by predators. Then there are the stick insects. They have long, skinny bodies and colors that make them look like twigs or branches, complete with movements like a branch swaying in the wind.

Spongy moths in South Korea can adapt their color and behavior to match local tree bark. To stay hidden in daylight, they often shuffle along the surface to find a spot that better matches their own coloration. Other insects have adapted to look like blotches of mold and lichen.

STEPHEN FRINK/GETTY IMAGES

THE COLOR OF SLOW MOTION

Slow-moving animals are vulnerable, so they need to come up with unique (and colorful) ways to survive. Snails are some of the slowest-moving animals of all, so they use shells to protect their soft bodies. The shells of Cuban painted snails add color as a distraction. How does that work? The bright reds, yellows, greens, blues, purples and pinks of their intricate designs make it difficult for some predators, like birds, to identify them all as snails. Even individual snails of the same species have differences in their patterns and colors. A few seconds of doubt in the natural world can mean the difference between life and death.

A tiny, slow-moving creature less than an inch (two centimeters) in size is easy pickings for predators, so the pygmy seahorse resorts to hiding between the corals. And it has another trick up its sleeve. Slowly, like a master painter, its color changes to match its coral host, even assuming textures that mimic the branches and polyps of the coral to fine-tune its disappearing act.

FAST-CHANGE ARTISTS

Intertidal pools are small bodies of water left on rocky shores when the tides recede. They can change quickly as the tides come in and go out. Many of the creatures in these pools, such as blennies and gobies, can change the darkness and lightness of their colors to stay hidden while seabirds and seals search the pools for food. The chameleon prawn can change from red to green when seaweed grows in the pools and back to red when it disappears as the tide goes out. Others take a different approach. The long-legged spider crab has little hooks on its body that snag the seaweed, creating what looks like a grass dress with long legs poking out. If you can't hide in the vegetation, then why not wear it? Hermit crabs borrow the abandoned shells of other animals to stay out of sight, even switching shells when the color and light of the pool changes.

SLOTH GREEN

The three-toed sloth sleeps upside down in the moist rainforest of South America. Its shaggy fur is fertile ground for algae, which flourish in the wet hairs and slowly turn the sloth green, keeping it hidden amid the foliage.

THE GREAT DECEIVERS

Disruptive camouflage is coloration and patterning that hide the outline of an animal's body. For example, the lime hawk-moth has pale pink wings. But the outer edges are lined with a green pattern that helps the moth blend into the forest background. It's all about disappearing quickly when you need to. At first glance you may not think that the white stripes on a zebra's black body could possibly hide them against the African landscape. But their bold patterns disrupt the outline of each individual animal, creating a kind of motion blur that makes it difficult for an attacking lion to target a weak individual, particularly with the whole herd on the run.

This lime hawk-moth almost disappears on a lichen-covered branch. The irregular patterns on its wings when spread and flattened also mimic the shadows and leaf veins of the vegetation in its habitat.
WIRESTOCK/GETTY IMAGES

Eyes are often dark and glossy, and they can draw attention to an animal's head. Many fish have evolved dark patches or bands around their eyes to reduce the contrast and confuse attacking predators. Eyespots found on the wings of butterflies like the monarch, the red admiral and the peacock also serve to distract and confuse predators. This ***defensive mimicry*** relies on the eyespots resembling the eyes of dangerous animals like owls or other raptors that are natural predators of the butterflies.

FLYING DRAGONS AND BLUE-TAILED SKINKS

No matter how well camouflaged an animal is, once it starts to move it becomes more visible to predators. Some reptiles have evolved colors to address this problem. In the mountainous rainforests of Southeast Asia, the *Draco* lizard, also known as the flying dragon, floats from tree to tree using flaps of skin that run between its front and hind limbs. To hide its fanciful flights, it has evolved colors and patterns on its wing flaps, ranging from mottled reds to yellows to various shades of forest greens. In addition, the lizard's flight pattern looks like leaves spiraling downward, helping to further disguise the flying lizard.

Another reptile, the blue-tailed skink in Australia, has evolved a bright blue tail that attracts the attention of an aggressor to its tail (rather than to its head or torso). Why? The blue tail breaks off easily, leaving the predator with a twitching tail and the skink with a chance to escape—tailless. Not to worry, though, because in a month or two, a brand-new blue tail will grow back again.

A *Draco* lizard's wings are rib extensions covered in bark-like scales on the outside, for camouflage, and brightly colored on the undersides. These colors are used to dominate rivals and for courtship displays.
NEAGONEFO/GETTY IMAGES

DO YOU SEE WHAT I SEE?

A Bengal tiger is a colorful animal in the grasslands and rainforests of India, with its bright orange fur and jagged black stripes. The tiger is one of the fiercest hunters and most powerful predators on Earth. But how does it manage to stay out of sight while hunting deer? Well, it turns out that the deer have no red receptors in their eyes—they cannot see orange or red. To the deer, the tiger appears a dull green color, its dark stripes blending into the tall spiky grasses of its habitat. Notably, tigers have no red receptors either, so they cannot see the rich orange color of their own coats.

Biologists are working with wildlife photographers using special color and UV filters to get a closer look at how animals see each other and the environment they live in. For example, a yellow filter placed over the lens of the camera removes all the orange light, recording more accurately how the tiger and deer see in the wild.

The blue-tailed skink can move at lightning speed when it needs to avoid predators, darting under logs or into crevices. Its natural body color helps it stay hidden when it's motionless.
BUDDY MAYS/GETTY IMAGES

Bengal tigers recognize each other by their stripe patterns, which are unique to each individual. Tigers have white eyespots on the backs of their ears that may scare off rivals even when the tiger is walking away.
MANUEL ROMARIS/GETTY IMAGES

SEASONAL OUTFITS

What do you do if your lush, green grassland home changes to a cold, snowy landscape? You put on a winter coat, right? Arctic foxes, hares and weasels also have coats, and the colors adjust to the changing seasons. As the days get shorter and colder, animals produce hormones that affect hair growth and pigmentation. As a result, their fur gets thicker, melanin production stops, and the fur changes to white, providing them with warmth and camouflage in the snowy landscape. Even birds can get into the magical coat act. The ptarmigan is a grouse that spends a lot of its time on the ground in the Arctic. Every fall it loses its summer feathers and grows brand-new white plumage, the perfect camouflage for the snowy Arctic tundra. These seasonal changes don't happen overnight, and sometimes

This arctic fox, seen in a field of lupines in Alaska, is still changing to its summer coat. Its fur also thins out to prevent overheating as Arctic temperatures rise.
JOHNNY JOHNSON/GETTY IMAGES

The red mark above this Arctic ptarmigan's eye, called an eye comb, becomes more vivid during spring breeding season, acting as a sign of dominance in males. The eye comb shrinks back in the winter, helping the bird remain hidden in the snow.
KARL ANDER ADAMI/GETTY IMAGES

the snow melts before the ptarmigan can transition back to its summer plumage. Some researchers have seen ptarmigans rolling around in the mud. They believe the birds are darkening their white feathers, which they have not yet molted because spring is arriving earlier due to the climate crisis.

THE COLOR OF PREDATION

Animals use color in their skin, feathers and scales for more than camouflage and mating. Evolution has provided them with many ways to protect themselves from predators. Color is a valuable defense and it does not always involve hiding from those who want to eat you for lunch.

The zebra's black and white stripes create a dazzling visual effect on predators such as lions, making it difficult for them to target individuals in a herd on the run. The stripes also play a role in temperature regulation (they produce tiny cooling air currents) and pest reduction (flies don't like the stripes).
GRANT ORDELHEIDE/GETTY IMAGES

5

DEFENSE: WARNINGS, DECEPTIONS AND CONFUSION

Animals defend themselves by using color as a warning to surprise, startle, deceive and even confuse their aggressors. The physical characteristics and behaviors that enable them to do this have evolved over millions of years.

THE "DON'T TOUCH ME" DEFENSE

The colors and patterns of many animals send a warning message to predators: "Watch out. I'm toxic!" This type of color-based defense is known as ***aposematism.*** Probably the most famous example is the wasp with its bright yellow and black stripes—a clear warning of its dangerous stinger. This same combination of yellow and black has become a global warning symbol, labeling electrical hazards, danger zones on roads and construction sites, and the police tape that surrounds crime scenes. The bluntness of the message is clear: "Stay away."

When the blue-ringed octopus is threatened, specialized cells in its skin rapidly change color, and bright blue rings light up and pulsate all over its body. If predators don't get the warning message, the octopus delivers its neurotoxin with a quick bite!
GIORDANO CIPRIANI/GETTY IMAGES

Another animal, small enough to fit in the palm of your hand and weighing just over half an ounce (15 grams), uses colors other than yellow and black yet is equally effective in sending a clear warning to predators. The blue-ringed octopus lives in the waters off Australia and emits a poison 1,000 times more deadly than cyanide, capable of killing several dozen people. In its resting state this octopus is light brown, but when threatened it develops 50 to 60 small, pulsating, neon-blue rings all over its body. Its poison is used to paralyze prey like crabs, fish and other crustaceans.

NINO_FOTOS/GETTY IMAGES

TINY BUT TOXIC

Some ***arachnids***, like black widow spiders, have well-placed warning colors on their bodies to announce the presence of their chemical weapons. These venomous spiders have a red hourglass mark imprinted on their undersides. Since they spend a lot of time hanging upside down near their webs, the placement of this mark helps keep the colored warning message highly visible to predators and yet somewhat hidden to unsuspecting victims that become entangled in their sticky, messy webs.

FRIEND OR FOE?

Snakes often use their colors and patterns to hide themselves on their hunting grounds. **Vipers** are venomous snakes with triangular-shaped heads who use poison to both defend themselves and immobilize their prey. Vipers are born with the ability to produce venom, so they are protected as soon as they emerge. Their bold zigzag patterns are a warning signal to potential predators. Coral snakes are also venomous, but they use bands of bright yellow, red and black to announce the presence of nerve toxins that paralyze their prey.

In the southern United States there is an old saying that goes "Red on yella, kill a fella. Red on black, a friend of Jack." This folk saying was meant to save people from deadly coral snakes, and it is relatively accurate as long as you are in North America. But be careful! Coral snakes found in Asia have different color patterns. Red on black is *not* "a friend of Jack"! So check the colors before you make this snake mistake.

The heavy-bodied Gaboon viper from Kenya mimics the colors of dead leaves and forest-floor debris with a disruptive (noncontinuous) pattern to hide itself while hunting rodents, birds and small mammals.

R. ANDREW ODUM/GETTY IMAGES

HOW TO STARTLE A PREDATOR

Color can be shocking at times, especially when it's not expected. It can cause aggressors to take a step back, opening an escape route for the animal under threat. The green flash of the crystal jellyfish can startle marine animals much bigger than itself, making them hesitate or retreat and increasing the jellyfish's chances of survival. Bright colors can also be used to surprise predators.

COLOR CLUE

BACKUP PLANS

The shield bug backs up its bright red warning message to birds and other predators with a foul-smelling liquid released from its rear end. That should make aggressors back up!

A garden tiger moth perches on a lichen-covered rock. Its forewings look like dead leaves or bark, keeping it hidden when at rest. Its black-spotted orange hind wings warn predators that it is toxic.
MIKE POWLES/GETTY IMAGES

For example, the garden tiger moth has a dark gray-and-cream pattern on its forewings that provides camouflage when it's at rest. Bright orange, black-spotted hind wings act as a hidden defense system if the moth is attacked by a bird. An on-off startle defense is more common and proves more effective in butterflies and moths that have large wing surfaces of 2.5 to 3.5 inches (6.5 to 9 centimeters), such as the eyed hawk-moth. Although it is well camouflaged in its resting position, this giant moth flashes red and blue eyespots on its hind wings when predators approach, startling them and giving the moth a chance to make a quick escape.

BUG BULLETIN

Ladybirds, beetles known in North America as ladybugs, are well known for the vibrant red, orange, yellow and black spotted patterns on their bodies and wings. The seven-spot ladybird is the most common species among a whopping 3,500 species spread around the world. Their bright colors warn predators that they contain toxic chemicals. If predators don't get the message, the beetles have a backup plan. They ooze out a smelly yellow liquid from their leg joints in a process known as reflex bleeding. The ladybugs get pigmented colors from their food by ingesting carotenoids along with substances that combine to build their toxins. Brighter reds and yellows in ladybug patterns signal the presence of more toxins to predatorial birds, encouraging them to choose duller-colored beetles. Ladybug moms try to protect their babies from the start by passing on toxins to their eggs.

DOMENICO SCALZO/
GETTY IMAGES

Female cuckoos lay speckled blue eggs in European robins' nests, mimicking the colors and patterns of their host's eggs. If the cuckoo's egg is a good match, the robin is tricked into raising the chick that hatches from it.
JOHN NAVAJO/SHUTTERSTOCK.COM

GREAT DECEPTIONS

Evolution, it seems, favors a good con artist. Some species of cuckoo birds are brood parasites—they download their motherly chores onto another bird. Here's how it works. The cuckoo female deposits one of her eggs in a robin's nest when the mother robin is not there. The match is not perfect—the cuckoo egg is slightly larger—but the colors and patterns are close enough to fool the mother robin. The cuckoo mothers go to great lengths *not* to work at motherhood. Some even push robin's eggs out of their nests to make room for their own. When the mother robin returns to the nest, she doesn't notice the intruder egg and takes care of it as if it were her own. The cuckoo chick is typically the first to emerge, and it quickly grows larger than the robin's chicks. Like mother, like child, this little impostor has also been observed ejecting robin's eggs (and sometimes the chicks) from the nest to ensure more food for itself.

FEED ME!

The wide-open mouths of many chicks are bright red inside to tell the parent birds, "Put food here!"

Some amphibians also deceive others by making themselves larger and more ferocious. How? With inflatable bodies! The Cuyaba dwarf frog in South America sits quietly tucked away in its habitat most of the time. But when it is threatened, this colorful creature inflates itself to over twice its size. Then it turns around to display two large black "false eyes" ringed with yellow on its rear end, making it look like a much larger and fiercer animal.

An owl butterfly perched on a tree trunk in Peru displays a large circular eyespot on its underwing that scares off predators like frogs, lizards and birds. The top side of this butterfly's wings are often colorful and are used to attract mates.
FRANS LEMMENS/GETTY IMAGES

LOOK LIKE A TOUGH GUY

Along with success come the copycats. That's the basis for ***Batesian mimicry***, when a harmless species mimics the warning signals of a larger, more dangerous animal to protect themselves—especially when the mimic is not dangerous at all.

- Wasps *are* dangerous, but the hoverfly mimic warns off predators with colors and stripes similar to wasps', even though it cannot sting at all.
- Viceroy butterflies mimic monarchs with wings decorated in similar colors and patterns—most predators mistake them for the foul-tasting monarchs and avoid them altogether.
- Owl butterflies in Costa Rica have large dark wings with eyespots that look like the eyes of an owl—enough to scare off birds and other predators.
- Caterpillars can also use mimicry for defense, but hawk-moth caterpillars take it to the extreme. They raise up their rear ends and bend their bodies into the triangular shape of a viper's head. Astonishingly, they have two large spots located exactly where the snake's eyes would be. Most birds and other predators won't go near them, fearing a venomous viper's bite.

A small bluestreak cleaner wrasse attends to a yellow boxfish in a win-win, mutually beneficial relationship. The boxfish gets its parasites removed, and the wrasse, identified by its bright blue streaks, gets food and protection from the much larger fish.
HANSGERTBROEDER/GETTY IMAGES

CHICK CONS AND MARINE MIMICS

Now this one is truly weird: a bird that mimics a caterpillar. Seriously? Young chicks are at the most vulnerable stage of their bird lives, so of course that's when snakes and carnivorous birds try to make them tasty morsels. The cinereous mourner is a bird of a rather dull gray-brown color that lives in the lowland forests of South America. Surprisingly, its chicks are covered in downy bright orange hair with white spots. Strange? Well, they look very similar to the local tussock moth caterpillar that has stinging hairs all over its body. When threatened, the chicks bob their little heads up and down just like the caterpillars do—a form of behavioral mimicry.

The bluestreak cleaner wrasse is well known for its services in coral reef cleaning stations. Many fish allow the wrasse to approach and clean off their pesky parasites. The devious blenny fish, however, has learned to take advantage of these friendly relationships by changing its brown stripes to blue stripes using specialized color cells. The blenny, pretending to be a cleaner wrasse, then approaches unsuspecting fish, who often end up with bite marks from the blenny's sharp teeth. This type of behavior is known as aggressive mimicry. No kidding!

The bright colors of this sea slug are a warning to predators of the toxins it ingests from eating sea sponges. The orange antennae-like protrusions are called rhinophores, and they help the slug both "smell" and feel its way around.
KHAICHUIN SIM/GETTY IMAGES

DON'T DINE HERE

Slugs? Yuck! They're slimy, gray and gooey, and they hide in dark, damp places. Right? Wrong! Sea slugs are some of the most colorful animals on Earth. Often called nudibranchs, they live on ocean floors, where they gobble up fallen organic debris. Their small, soft bodies, only two inches (five centimeters) in size, make a tasty treat for predators, so many species arm themselves with toxins absorbed from a diet of anemone and sponges. Some slugs also have poisonous, stinging appendages, but it is their vibrant colors, appearing like neon signs along a dark highway, that announce their "don't dine here" message. One particularly toxic slug, the yellow-plumed sea slug, releases sulfuric acid when threatened. Some of the bright colors also camouflage the sea slugs against the colorful coral reef seafloor.

BITTER BIRDS, NEWT BELLIES AND GILA MONSTERS

Poisonous birds? Really? Yes, they exist, although they weren't widely known until recently. They include red warblers in Mexico, and the blue-capped ifrit and the highly poisonous hooded pitohui from New Guinea. The pitohui, with its red, brown and black skin and feathers, contains a powerful toxin called batrachotoxin, the same neurotoxin that's in the poison dart frog. The pitohui's diet contains a group of flower beetles that are on the dart frog's favorite snack list too.

The rough-skinned newt is a North American amphibian with rather unremarkable dark brown skin. But when it is threatened by a predator such as a garter snake, this unusual creature curls its head and tail upward, revealing a bright orange underbelly. If the snake still chooses to take a bite, it gets a mouthful of tetrodotoxin—one of the most powerful neurotoxins on Earth and the same poison found in the blue-ringed octopus.

Reptiles also send colored warnings to predators. The Gila monster, found in the deserts of the United States and Mexico, lumbers around confidently in broad daylight, and not just because of its imposing size. This venomous lizard's bright pink or orange patterns scare off predators, who know of the venom the monster's teeth can deliver. My motto? Never look a Gila monster in the face—no matter how colorful it is!

The colors and patterns on the body of the venomous Gila monster are a signal to most predators to back away. In rocky habitats the colors provide camouflage when the reptile is at rest.
MILAN ZYGMUNT/GETTY IMAGES

TO A COLORFUL FUTURE

What a glorious world we live in, and what a privilege it is to be sharing it with so many amazing colorful animals. But history shows us that people have ravaged landscapes, clear-cut forests, mined deep into the earth for coal and precious minerals, drilled for oil and natural gas, and hunted wild animals for their meat or just for the sport of it. And as of more recent times, uniquely colored animals are being overharvested to supply the global pet trade.

With your help we can change our relationship with this living, breathing planet. The more we know about the colorful animals that live near us in the wild and in our cities and countryside, the more we will protect and care for them. From knowledge grows love and respect. This is the best way to conserve wildlife and live in harmony with the natural world.

Mucus on the body of the clownfish protects it from the stinging cells of the anemone. The bright colors of the fish also act as a clear territorial defense signal to intruders, saying, "This is my home, stay out!"
STRMKO/GETTY IMAGES

6

CONSERVING NATURE'S PALETTE

Colorful animals are affected by the common threats of habitat loss, the climate crisis, pesticides, and light and sound pollution. Dark-colored animals absorb more heat from sunlight than light-colored animals do. In hot regions of the world, this can lead to animals overheating more quickly, reducing their survival rates as temperatures rise due to the climate crisis. Will natural selection result in the evolution of animals with lighter skin, scales and feathers to offset the extreme heat in ecosystems near the equator? Or will these animals have to change behavioral patterns by seeking more shade, being more active at night or moving to cooler habitats? How do we monitor these changes? These are some of the questions facing conservationists as we move into the future on a warming planet.

EXOTIC ANIMALS AT HOME

Parrots, macaws and cockatiels, chameleons, poison dart frogs, geckos, bearded dragons, tarantulas and snakes, betta, mandarin and clownfish, Cuban painted snails and crabs—these are some of the more popular species in the pet and aquarium trades. Exotic species are very popular with pet buyers, so collectors can demand higher prices and bring in more profit. This can result in increased illegal harvesting, making it difficult to monitor and conserve wild populations in remote areas.

Geckos are popular in the pet trade. Each animal has a unique personality, and geckos are low maintenance. Captive-bred geckos supply most pet stores, easing the impact on wild populations.
NATASHA LAZARIDI/GETTY IMAGES

GIRAFFES IN A SPOT

If your neck is 8 feet (2.4 meters) long and you live in an open savanna, hiding yourself from predators like lions becomes a major problem. The unique brown jigsaw-like patterns on a giraffe's body serve as a form of camouflage. But recent research shows that the intensity of its colors play a role in male dominance. Dark orange-brown colors indicate strength, higher testosterone levels and a healthy male who is more likely to father strong offspring. Younger, less-dominant male giraffes who are lighter in color tend to avoid physical battles with dominant males. Heat-sensitive cameras show that the large spots also act as cooling patches, radiating heat away from the giraffe's body in the hot savanna summers. Darker-colored giraffes tend to get hotter, but they also filter out damaging solar radiation better. How will color dominance change in giraffe populations in a warming world? As temperatures rise due to the climate crisis, will these wonderfully unique creatures be able to survive?

BISCUT/GETTY IMAGES

The rainbow lorikeet is a popular pet. But lorikeets have a very specialized diet in the wild, consisting of pollen, nectar and fruit, that is hard to replicate in captivity. These highly active social birds need a lot of interaction to stay healthy.
AIRE IMAGES/GETTY IMAGES

PETS ON THE MOVE

The transporting of animals collected for the pet trade can be extremely stressful for the animals, especially when conditions are less than ideal. Physical injuries from rough handling, overcrowding and poor nutrition and hydration are common for animals in transit. Ownership is often short-lived, since many pet owners do not know how to care for these unusual animals. As a result, many animals either die or are released into the wild.

Although the pet trade can provide an income for local communities, the collecting and transporting of animals needs stricter regulation to be sustainable. The males of many species are favored by pet buyers, as they often have the most vibrant colors (like the scarlet macaw and the eclectus parrot). But removing a lot of males from a wild population quickly leads to lower reproduction rates, particularly for those species with small populations or limited distribution ranges.

Public education programs need to encourage responsible consumer behavior. Enforcement of harvesting restrictions requires cooperation between the countries where the animals live and the countries where they are being purchased.

EASING THE PRESSURE

When animals are at extreme risk of going extinct, scientists and zookeepers take some into captivity to care for them and help them have babies. This is known as captive breeding. It is important for the well-being of the animals that these facilities have enclosures that are as similar as possible to natural habitats. Also, the breeding animals need to have lots of differences in their genes (known as broad genetic diversity) to keep their immune systems strong and their populations healthy. If the animals are too closely related, they can pass on bad genes that make offspring weaker and more likely to get sick. Once there are enough healthy animals in a breeding program, some are released back into the wild. But it's still important to protect their natural homes so that they have a safe place to live.

Aquariums can give us an emotional connection to marine and freshwater environments by allowing us to witness the movements, sounds and interactions of the animals. They can raise awareness of the challenges the animals face in the wild and the need to protect them.
DAMIRCUDIC/GETTY IMAGES

COLOR CLUE

WILD PAINTERS

Vincent van Crow was a rescue crow who painted with a brush held in his beak and became a model for animal-enrichment painting programs. There are now painting elephants, giraffes (the canvases must be huge), sea lions (hmm...I wonder if they paint with those whiskers) and macaws (after all, you can never have *too* much color!).

Once a kestrel spots prey, it quickly pounces. It can adapt to urban environments, but pesticides and habitat loss are threats to wild populations.
PAUL MCMULLEN/GETTY IMAGES

IN THE FOOTSTEPS OF VINCENT VAN CROW

I love this story! Kestrels are the most colorful falcons, the males with black-spotted bellies, a reddish-brown back and tail feathers, and blue-gray heads. They also have two eyespots on their backs, placed to deceive songbirds that mob the falcons in an attempt to defend their nests and offspring. Kestrel populations are declining—there are now about half as many in the wild as there were 50 years ago (a loss of two million birds).

Ferrisburgh, a rescued kestrel at a nature center and wildlife rehabilitation center in Vermont, is recovering from injuries. Birds are meant to fly freely, so being in an enclosure can be difficult for them. To help manage his mental health, keepers taught Ferrisburgh how to paint. He couldn't hold a paintbrush in his curved beak (all raptors have curved beaks), so with his feet covered in multicolored bird-friendly paint, he runs across a prepared canvas, creating colorful tracks. The results are modern abstract paintings, no doubt inspired by mealworm snacks placed on the opposite side of the canvas by the keepers (after all, artists need to eat too!). The "Coloring with Kestrels" family program let visitors paint along with Ferrisburgh and learn about falcon ecology and conservation at the same time.

PETS GONE WILD

Pet owners who can't or don't want to take care of their animals anymore sometimes release them into the wild. This can create environmental problems. Here's an example. Apple snails, native to the wetlands of Argentina, are colorful creatures, making them popular with aquarium owners. They reproduce hundreds of bright pink globular eggs that look like cotton candy on a stick. Those eggs are packed with poison, their pink color warning predators, "Eat at your own risk." Animals that do eat them are unable to digest the toxic compounds. If owners release them the snails can spread into local waterways through rivers and streams. They have damaged native water plants in Florida and devastated rice fields in Southeast Asia and Africa. Like all invasive species that have no local predators, the snails cause problems for native plants and animals by outcompeting them for natural resources. And they're not the only pet-trade animals to do so.

- Burmese pythons and boa constrictors released by pet owners who can no longer manage them are threatening native animals in the Florida Everglades.
- Green iguanas from Central and South America have spread diseases and damaged native vegetation in Florida and other places where they have no natural predators.
- The African clawed frog has become an invasive species competing against native amphibians that are already impacted by a dangerous virus and droughts brought on by the climate crisis.

Burmese pythons are one of the most popular pythons in the pet trade because of their striking colors and typically quiet nature. Poaching can lead to overexploitation in the wild and decrease wild populations already struggling with habitat loss and climate change.
KRISTIAN BELL/GETTY IMAGES

Wildfires are devastating to forest biodiversity, especially when they reach protected areas and wildlife refuges that have been set up to protect unique and vulnerable species. The spread of disease increases in the aftermath of these fires.
PATRICK ORTON/GETTY IMAGES

ALONE WITHOUT A HOME

Every wild animal needs a home. But frequent wildfires are burning more intensely and swallowing larger and larger areas of forest, forcing wildlife out of their homes. Many die when they are trapped by the fires, and those that survive often have no place to go. Every year in North America, an area the size of 10 million football fields is lost to forest fires. Carefully managing forests by clearing dry plants and undergrowth that easily catch fire can help prevent large fires. We also need to plant more trees and protect forests to help them recover and provide homes for animals again.

Conservationists around the world are concerned about tropical rainforests, as they are the "lungs" of our planet, providing 20 percent of the world's oxygen. They are also home to over half of Earth's animal and plant species, including many of the colorful birds, amphibians and reptiles mentioned in this book.

Indigenous Peoples need to be included in conservation programs. They have an intimate knowledge of the land which they live on and this includes a tradition of sustainable living. The Emberá and Chocó Peoples in Colombia and Panama collect poison dart frogs and, without harming them, gently rub their backs to extract the poison for the tips of their blowgun darts and arrows. They then release them back into the wild. These Indigenous groups hunt only birds and other small prey with their darts, but habitat destruction is threatening their way of life as well as the dart-frog populations.

The main threat to the blue poison dart frog is deforestation, which results in loss of its delicate habitat. The climate crisis has meant changes in temperature and rainfall patterns.

OLEG KOVTUN HYDROBIO/SHUTTERSTOCK.COM

GALÁPACOLORS

The Galápagos Islands are famous for inspiring Charles Darwin's theory of evolution by natural selection. They are now under threat from rising sea levels, endangering the islands' iguanas, giant tortoises and colorful birds.

HOT COLOR CRISIS

Colorful lizards and snakes that live in desert regions are threatened by rising temperatures that are making their habitats unlivable. Island habitats are also in danger, due to rising ocean levels caused by melting glaciers and other effects of the climate crisis. Island wildlife is often made up of colorful exotic species that have evolved in isolation for hundreds of thousands of years. They will have nowhere to go as island coastlines erode, reducing the size of their habitat and placing them high on the International Union for Conservation of Nature's list of species of concern.

Head for the mountains, you say? Not so fast! Mountain habitats are like islands in the sky. Many mountain species, such as the American pika, a small rabbit-like mammal that lives within limited temperature ranges, are moving to higher, cooler altitudes as global temperatures rise. Unfortunately, their food sources are often unable to move with them. What will happen to these species when they reach the top of the mountain, with nowhere else to go?

The American pika is highly sensitive to temperature changes, in part because it does not hibernate and is active year-round. High-altitude habitats are shrinking due to the climate crisis. Expanding protected areas is important for this small mammal.
JAMIE LAMB/GETTY IMAGES

A green sea turtle swims over a healthy coral reef in Egypt. A weakened coral reef ecosystem reduces the number of places where fish can hide, breed and graze, making survival more difficult for species like the algae-eating yellow tang.
GEORGETTE DOUWMA/GETTY IMAGES

NOBODY LIKES A COLORLESS REEF

Many of the most colorful marine animals live in or near coral reefs that are threatened by warming ocean waters. The algae that give corals their bright colors and energy are very sensitive to heat. When the water gets too hot, the algae die, causing the coral to turn white (called coral bleaching), and eventually the corals die.

Unregulated harvesting of fish and other animals can also damage the coral structures, and the removal of animals or groups of animals can upset ecosystem balance and lead to the loss of genetic diversity. Harmful methods of harvesting include cyanide poisoning, which stuns the fish for easier collection and kills other animals nearby. Blast fishing is even worse—it uses explosions that stun or kill large schools of fish, at the same time destroying parts of the reef and other marine life. Though these practices are banned in many countries, they are still used in some regions.

THE SOUND OF COLORLESS CRABS

Sound pollution in the ocean, caused by boats, blasting and drilling, makes it hard for sea animals like whales, dolphins and porpoises to communicate, find food and navigate. Crabs are crustaceans that also rely on ***echolocation*** to navigate the seabed. Recent research in the United Kingdom indicates that the crabs are affected by noise from passing ships. Young juvenile shore crabs use hormones to adjust their light and dark colors, matching their bodies to the background of their environment for camouflage. Scientists collected crabs and exposed them in a lab setting to sounds similar to the invasive ship sounds. The researchers discovered that the crabs couldn't camouflage themselves or respond to predators as effectively, making them more vulnerable in their ocean habitat. Other natural environmental noises had no effect.

CLIFF LESERGENT/GETTY IMAGES

This NASA photo taken from space shows the artificial lights on Earth at night in Japan. Light pollution is disrupting the natural cycles and behavior of terrestrial and marine animals, particularly those that are nocturnal.

VISIBLE EARTH/NASA

ARTIFICIAL LIGHTS AND CHEMICALS

Too much of a good thing can become a problem. Photos from NASA satellites show us that our planet no longer sleeps in darkness at night—it is awash in light. This causes problems for many nocturnal animals. Colorful migratory birds have evolved to get their directions from the stars and moonlight, and they are confused by artificial lights. They are killed when they are attracted to and collide with brightly lit commercial buildings in our cities. Bright lights from highways discourage migratory birds from landing in once-wild places, contributing to exhaustion on their migrations and reducing their migratory ranges.

THE COLOR OF COOL

Cities are hot places, built with asphalt, concrete and other materials that absorb and retain heat. Scientists recently developed a super-white paint that reflects 98 percent of the sun's rays, cooling surfaces by as much as 8 degrees Fahrenheit (13 degrees Celsius), even in the direct rays of the hot sun. Painting it onto the roofs of buildings and other city surfaces may help cool hot cities in our warming world. Scientists are also working on special paints that don't fade even under strong sunlight or UV light like what airplanes and spacecraft face high up in the sky or in space. Structural colors don't damage the environment since they don't contain materials that are mined from the earth. An airplane sprayed with paint made from structural color can be up to a ton lighter than a plane painted with pigmented colors. This means lower fuel costs and lower emissions of the greenhouse gas carbon dioxide that contributes to global warming.

PRAPAT AOWSAKORN/SHUTTERSTOCK.COM

Coral reefs are affected by sky glow from nearby cities, leading to an imbalance of species and the loss of some colorful organisms. But we still have time to save the night. You can help by switching off the porch lights and changing blue LED lights to warm yellow. Light pollution damages habitats in many different ways.

Pesticides, chemicals and fertilizers applied to crops and gardens are devastating colorful insects and birds around the world. Many of these animals are pollinators, and their loss reduces crop production and food supplies and creates an imbalance in ecosystems.

A monarch butterfly visits a pink coneflower to feed on its nectar. It will subsequently spread the flower's pollen. The loss of its beloved milkweed habitat is devastating for the monarch's reproduction and migratory routes.
CAPPI THOMPSON/GETTY IMAGES

BE A COLORFUL CITIZEN

Is there an eco club at your school that you can join? Local environmental groups sometimes partner with schools. Is there one near you that might come and conduct an awareness session on biodiversity and ecosystems?

We need active participants to combat the climate crisis and protect the wild spaces and the colorful animals and plants that call them home. Is there a park or a trail nearby that offers an opportunity to adopt a section or area to keep clean and healthy and learn about the local wildlife? You may be surprised at how many colorful creatures there are right in your backyard.

Can you start a pollinator garden near your home? By choosing the plants carefully, you can create a garden that attracts colorful butterflies and birds.

Nature expeditions at school, summer camps and eco clubs create a lasting connection to the natural world and encourage active participation in conservation efforts.

FG TRADE/GETTY IMAGES

Consider building birdhouses to provide homes for local or migrating birds.

Are there community events near you where you can see displays and join an environmental organization that supports biodiversity? This is a wonderful way to meet scientists and learn some of the methods they use in their research.

Are there projects in which your whole family can participate? See if there are any citizen-scientist groups you can join.

Is there a bird-count project near you where you can help collect data to track changes in bird populations?

Birds are some of the most colorful animals on earth. Bird-watching is a wonderful way to observe them in their natural habitats and see firsthand how diverse and interconnected the natural world is.
PEOPLEIMAGES/GETTY IMAGES

On your next walk through the woods, record the number of different natural colors in plants and animals you encounter. Make your connection to the natural world of color, and you may soon be the one telling your friends all about it.

GLOSSARY

adaptive evolution—a process by which species develop traits over time, through natural selection, that help them survive in a particular habitat

algae—photosynthetic organisms that grow in aquatic environments, ranging from single-celled microscopic forms to multicellular structures like seaweed

aposematism—an animal's behavior and traits, such as bright colors, markings, chemical emissions or sounds, that warn predators to stay away

arachnids—organisms without a spine, with four pairs of jointed legs and several body parts, a group that includes spiders, scorpions and ticks

Batesian mimicry—the behavior of a harmless species that mimics the warning signals of a larger, more dangerous animal to avoid being attacked by predators

biochemistry—the study of the tiny building blocks of life, molecules like proteins, DNA and other chemicals, that keep living things alive

bioluminescent—quality of an organism that produces and emits its own light made from chemical reactions in its own body

camouflage—the use of color, pattern and texture to hide or disguise an animal in its environment

carotenoids—a class of pigments responsible for red, yellow and orange colors, chemicals that help algae and other plants in the process of photosynthesis

chromatophores—pigment-containing cells found in the skin of many animals

cyanophores—specialized pigment cells that reflect blue light

defensive mimicry—the use of color and design on an animal's body to make it look like a more dangerous animal or like other things in nature

dichromatic vision—seeing the world with only two colors instead of the full rainbow

disruptive camouflage—the use of color and pattern by an animal to break up the outline of its shape, making it difficult for predators and prey to see them

echolocation—a method of navigation whereby an animal such as a bat or a dolphin emits sounds and then listens to the echoes to determine where those objects are located in its environment

gametes—reproductive cells that unite during sexual reproduction to produce a new organism

harem—a group of female animals associated with a single male

infrared light—long-wavelength light emitted by the sun, fires and living organisms, detected by some animals with specialized heat-sensitive organs

iridescent—displaying shimmering colors as the angle of the viewer or the angle of the light striking the surface changes, as in the feathers of many birds

keratin—a strong structural protein that is the main component of finger- and toenails, feathers, horns and claws

lichen—a composite organism that consists of a delicate balance between fungi and algae, capable of surviving in extreme environments

nanocrystals—tiny crystals that are 1 to 100 nanometers in size (a nanometer is one billionth of a meter)

pigmentation—natural color in an animal's skin or other tissues due to the presence of molecules that reflect and absorb certain wavelengths of light

polarized light—light that travels in one plane, creating strong reflections for the viewer

sexual dimorphism—observable physical differences between males and females of the same species, such as size, shape and color

ultraviolet light—light that has a wavelength shorter than humanly visible light but that many animals can see

vipers—venomous snakes with triangular shaped-heads containing heat-sensitive pits and long, hinged fangs that inject poison into their prey

wavelength—a property of light, the distance between two peaks in a wave, usually measured in nanometers (nm).

RESOURCES

PRINT

Arnosky, Jim. *Hidden Wildlife: How Animals Hide in Plain Sight*. Union Square Kids, 2017.

Duprat, Guillaume. *Eye Spy: Wild Ways Animals See the World*. What on Earth!, illustrated edition, 2018.

Gish, Melissa. *Chameleons* (Living Wild). Creative Paperbacks, 2023.

Jenkins, Steve. *Eye to Eye: How Animals See the World*. Clarion Books, 2014.

Johnson, Rebecca L. *Masters of Disguise: Amazing Animal Tricksters*. Millbrook Press, 2018.

Park, Jane. *Hidden Animal Colors*. Millbrook Press, 2022.

Perdew, Laura. *Animal Survival: Working Together to Survive*. North Star Editions, 2022.

Ridley, Kimberly. *Extreme Survivors: Animals That Time Forgot*. Tilbury House, 2019.

Stevens, Martin. *Life in Colour: How Animals See the World*. BBC Books, 2021.

Stevens, Martin, and Sami Merilaita, eds. *Animal Camouflage: Mechanisms and Function*. Cambridge University Press, illustrated edition, 2011.

ONLINE

National Geographic Kids, Wacky Weekend: Hidden Animals: kids.nationalgeographic.com/wacky-weekend/article/hidden-animals

Smithsonian Institution, Suited for Survival: nationalzoo.si.edu/education/school-programs/suited-survival

VIDEOS

"Animal Camouflage: Learn How Animals Can Blend In with Their Environments." Learn Bright YouTube Channel.

Animals with Cameras series. BBC Earth YouTube Channel.

Dancing with the Birds. Silverback Films, 2019.

"How to See Like an Animal." BBC Earth Kids YouTube Channel.

Life in Colour. Humble Bee Films and SeaLight Pictures, 2021.

"Perfect Camouflage" (*Wild Ones*, episode 9). Free Documentary—Nature YouTube Channel.

Super Hummingbirds. PBS America YouTube Channel.

Tiny Creatures. Blackfin, Ember and Momentum Content, 2020.

"Unveiling Nature's Palette: Surprising Animal Colors!" COOHESIVE YouTube Channel.

ACKNOWLEDGMENTS

A broad palette of brilliant people have helped bring the initial inspiration for this book into solid form. Thank you to Kirstie Hudson and Georgia Bradburne, my editors at Orca. I hope I wasn't too colorful for you in my first drafts. Thanks to Troy Cunningham, the designer at Orca, for making this book as visually stunning as the subject deserves. Orca, you make beautiful books!

Special thanks to my agent, Stacey Kondla at The Rights Factory, for keeping my writing life inspired, giving me feedback when I desperately need it and nerding out with me as I explore exciting new subjects and ideas.

To Reta for her harmonious color sense and her delight in all things colorful. I am also grateful to colorful India for welcoming my many visits and revealing your ancient treasures. Thank you to all my friends for listening patiently to my stories whether they wanted to or not. I also want to thank all of my art instructors through the years, who awakened the color centers in my eyes and brain and made me appreciate the subtle things that make art and the natural world more exciting.

Finally, my thanks to all the colorful creatures who make our planet brilliant and exciting by adding your own unique hues to nature's palette.

INDEX

Page numbers in **bold** *indicate an image caption.*

STEPHEN AITKEN is a biologist, an artist and an author/illustrator of picture books and nonfiction and environmental fiction for middle-grade readers all over the world. He is the cofounder and executive secretary of Biodiversity Conservancy International, a Canadian-based charity that restores degraded habitats, educates the young at heart and conducts biodiversity research. Stephen is the editorial director of *Biodiversity*, a peer-reviewed science journal published in partnership with Taylor & Francis in Oxfordshire, UK. His hometown is Ottawa, but Stephen maintains a studio in the Himalayas that he shares with several bashful geckos, an odd orange-eared mouse (that's a whole other story) and a very friendly mongoose who keeps the venomous vipers at bay.